WELCOME SPEECHES

WELCOME SPEECHES

And Emergency Addresses for All Occasions

by
HERSCHEL H. HOBBS

ZONDERVAN
PUBLISHING HOUSE OF THE ZONDERVAN CORPORATION
GRAND RAPIDS, MICHIGAN 49506

WELCOME SPEECHES
Copyright 1960 by
Zondervan Publishing House
Grand Rapids, Michigan

ISBN 0-310-26151-1

Printed in the United States of America

83   84   85   86   87   88 — 30   29   28   27   26   25

Dedicated to
LYNNE
who is thrice welcome

PREFACE

Oh, what a little thing can turn
A heavy heart from sighs to song!
A smile can make the world less stern,
A word can cause the soul to burn
With glow of heaven, all night long.
—Anonymous

It is in this spirit that this little volume of welcome addresses is presented. The loneliest feeling ever is to be alone in a crowd. A cheery, appropriate word of welcome may bridge gaps and blend strangers into friends with a common purpose. It would be a strange host indeed who admitted guests to his home, yet never expressed delight in their presence. If this be true of individuals, how much more so is it the case in public gatherings.

It is a truism that first impressions are lasting ones. Therefore, in every gathering it is important that visitors receive a wholesome impression of the group. It is especially true in church meetings. When all of the trappings are removed, a church is basically a fellowship. Fellowships thrive on mutual friendship and interest. So this booklet is designed primarily for church situations.

In no sense is it exhaustive in its treatment. It would be impossible to anticipate all situations which may arise. Thus these are but suggestions which, we trust, will serve as guides toward meeting a specific need.

If this effort on our part can contribute toward making one person feel that he is *wanted*, then its purpose shall have been fulfilled.

HERSCHEL H. HOBBS

CONTENTS

CONTENTS

1

WELCOME TO MINISTERS

and Other Church Workers

A NEW PASTOR AND FAMILY

During its lifetime our church has known many significant occasions. But none is more noteworthy nor fraught with meaning than this day when we welcome to our hearts a new pastor and his family.

Under the guidance of God we have invited the Reverend Mr. _____ to become the undershepherd of our flock. We have asked him and his family to break tender ties with another people to come to us as strangers in a strange land. We do not ask that you will love us today as you loved those from whom you have come. But it is our firm resolve so to live and work with you that soon the same intimate ties will bind us together in the Christian love of a pastor and his people.

In asking you to become God's undershepherd for us we have placed upon you a tremendous responsibility. We ask you to be our pastor, rejoicing with us when we rejoice and weeping with us when we weep. When we look to you from the pew it will be with the unuttered cry, "Sir, we would see Jesus." Before you always on this pulpit will be the Holy Bible. From it we ask that you will make us wise unto salvation, that you will teach us, reprove us, correct us and instruct us in all things pertaining to righteousness. We pray that you will become God's overseer as you lead us in planning and performing the work of the Lord. We know that you will be an example unto the flock both in word and in deed.

In turn, in this newly formed relationship we have assumed like obligations. We shall take you and your family to our hearts. We would respect your rights as those of a normal Christian family. We shall keep you, our pastor, informed as to our specific pastoral needs. Our hearts shall be open to receive the messages which God shall give through you. By our prayers, words and deeds we shall encourage you as we match your leadership with our fellowship. In the words of the Apostle Paul, we would become your fellow-laborers, all of us belonging to God.

In so doing, it is our prayer and expectation that before long we shall come to know that depth of love and fellowship between pastor and people which is expressed in the words of another pastor, John Fawcett, about his relation to his people:

> Blest be the tie that binds
> Our hearts in Christian love;
> The fellowship of kindred minds
> Is like to that above.
>
> Before our Father's throne
> We pour our ardent prayers;
> Our fears, our hopes, our aims are one,
> Our comforts and our cares.
>
> We share our mutual woes,
> Our mutual burdens bear;
> And often for each other flows
> The sympathizing tear.
>
> When we asunder part,
> It gives us inward pain;
> But we shall still be joined in heart,
> And hope to meet again.

The Wife of a New Pastor

No greater privilege could be mine than that afforded me on behalf of us all as we welcome, not only to this meeting, but to our hearts, the wife of our new pastor, Mrs. _____ .

A successful pastorate, more often than not, rests upon the wife of the pastor. John Ruskin once wrote, "The buckling on of a knight's armor by his lady's hand was not a mere caprice of romantic fashion. It is the type of an eternal truth that the soul's armor is never set to the heart unless a woman's hand has braced it, and it is only when she braces it loosely that the honor of manhood fails."

Our pastor is a knight of God in spiritual armor. The success of his mission, humanly speaking, depends more upon his lady, his wife, than upon any other. Her love, counsel, prayers and encouragement will brace his armor well.

Your love for your husband is tempered by your love for God. We trust that it shall be made richer and stronger by our love for you.

We do not expect you to do the impossible. Your first duty, like ours, is to your family and your home. Thus we do not ask of you more in church duties than we ourselves are willing to assume. But in the mutual love which we all have for our homes, our church and our Lord we join hearts and hands.

> Oh, how skilful grows the hand
> That obeyeth love's command;
> It is the heart, and not the brain
> That to the highest doth attain,
> And he who follows love's behest
> Far exceedeth all the rest.
> —HENRY WADSWORTH LONGFELLOW

A FORMER PASTOR

(By Present Pastor)

One among many of the joys which are mine as your pastor is that which is afforded me today. It is my personal pleasure, and on your behalf, to welcome back to this pulpit one who has served with you and has wrought well. Need I tell you his name? For you know him and love him.

God has made your hearts wondrously large, endowing you with the capacity for many kinds of love. I rejoice in the abiding love which you have toward Brother _____ . If you did not love him, I would fear that you lacked the capacity to love me. The fact that you hold him dear to your hearts only proves your love for me and mine.

In a sense, when the Apostle Paul spoke to the Ephesian elders, he spoke as a former pastor (Acts 20:17ff.). So, borrowing his words I would direct them to our guest for this hour. As we recall your labors as the pastor of this church, several things come to mind.

You served the Lord with all humility of mind. Your compassionate heart often overflowed with tears, as amid many

13

trials you declared the whole counsel of God. Spending yourself without reservation, you were God's messenger both in this pulpit and from house to house. In so doing you heralded the gospel of grace as you called for repentance toward God, and faith toward our Lord Jesus Christ. Thus you are pure from the blood of all men.

Knowing that Christ purchased your flock with His own blood, you fed them as a shepherd. You were God's overseer as you directed and led in abundant labors for the Lord. In laying down the mantle of the Lord's undershepherd to this flock, you commended us to God and to the word of His grace. Among this people your example was a living parable of our Lord's words, "It is more blessed to give than to receive."

The fruits of your labor live on. Upon the foundation of your ministry, and of those who preceded you, we have endeavored to build. The blessings of God upon us today flow from the living foundation of your abiding labor of love. Truly you planted, we have endeavored to water, but God gives the increase.

So with gratitude and pleasure too deep for my feeble words to express, for myself and family, and for this entire church family of faith, I welcome you as once again we take you to our hearts. You are a brother beloved, a co-laborer in the Lord, and a friend!

A FORMER PASTOR'S WIFE

The wise writer of Proverbs 18:22 uttered this great truth, "Whoso findeth a wife findeth a good thing, and obtaineth favour of the Lord."

It is my privilege to welcome to us one who is a personification of this sublime truth. If you would look for tangible evidence of this it will not be found written in the business minutes or public notices with regard to our church. Nor will you discover it in the news columns or the pictures of our local newspapers. You will find it written on the tables of our hearts.

As the queen of the parsonage you made it for your husband a refuge from the many trials and cares of a busy ministry. You shared both his dreams and his problems. Your wise counsel reflected itself in the increased effectiveness of his pulpit ministry. You were mother to his children — and sometimes father, too.

14

To paraphrase the words of another: You were the pastor's silent partner. You were not "called," but you came; not "installed" yet you served. You were an "ambassador-without-portfolio." You were "104 sermons a year" — on the listening end. You were our pastor's "beloved critic, counselor, confronter." You had "all the problems a minister has — plus him!" You were "wife, mother, cook, laundress, seamstress, chauffer — the Chancellor of the Exchequer — purchasing agent *par excellence.*" You were a woman with stars in your eyes and your hands in the dish pan.*

You never imposed yourself upon us, but were always available. You listened to our problems, yet kept our confidence inviolate. You walked with a quiet, sure tread, yet you left your footprints upon the sands of our lives.

So with joy we receive you to ourselves once again. You may be our former pastor's wife, but you are our friend forevermore.

A New Minister of Religious Education and Family

Basic in our religion is the element of teaching. In the Old Testament God commanded the children of Israel to teach. "Gather the people together, men, and women, and children, and thy stranger that is within thy gates, that they may hear, and that they may learn, and fear the Lord your God, and observe to do all the words of this law: And that their children, which have not known any thing, may hear, and learn to fear the Lord your God, as long as ye live in the land . . ." (Deuteronomy 31:12, 13).

When Jesus came He was known as the Teacher. His commission to His church was to teach all nations. Our church is committed to a teaching ministry with the Bible as its textbook.

In the providence of God we have invited Brother _____ to lead us in an expanding program of religious education. It is our delightful privilege to welcome him and his family to our hearts today.

We do not ask that you work for us but with us. Our task is your task. Your problems will be our concern. When we succeed we shall share with you the glory. When we fail we shall not ask that you bear all the blame.

*See "What Is a Minister's Wife?" Mrs. H. D. Brown, copyright 1959 by Outlook Publishers.

15

Ours are willing people. They do not need to be driven but led. Their hearts are large. As they love their pastor, so shall they love you. We shall not look upon you as a competitor but as a companion. As Aaron multiplied the usefulness of his brother, Moses, so will you enlarge the ministry of your Christian brother, our pastor.

In receiving you as our co-laborer we pledge to you our prayers. We stand ready to submit our time and talents as instruments of righteousness to be made more skillful in your hands. We do not ask you to do our work, but to show us how we may better perform it.

In the knowledge that the field is white unto harvest, and in recognition that the laborers are too few, we join you in prayer that the Lord of the harvest will send forth laborers into His harvest. And with you we are ready for God to answer our prayers through us.

A NEW MINISTER OF MUSIC AND FAMILY

Herbert Spencer once said that "music must rank as the highest of fine arts — as the one which, more than any other, ministers to human welfare." It is the universal language of the soul. It expresses the deepest longings of the human heart. By it man's noblest aspirations find expression. It comforts in sorrow. It exhilarates in joy. It summons to duty. When all other means of expression fail, it breaks forth in utter abandon, releasing the soul to flight into ethereal realms.

The Christian religion is a singing religion. David was the sweet singer of Israel. It was with joyful song that the angelic choir announced the birth of the Son of David, our Saviour. Jesus blended His voice with those of His disciples as, closing the first observance of the Last Supper, they sang a song and went out unto the Mount of Olives. Paul admonishes us to ". . . be filled with the Spirit; Speaking to yourselves in psalms and hymns and spiritual songs, singing and making melody in your heart to the Lord" (Ephesians 5:19).

Following the example of our Lord, and heeding the admonition of His apostle, our church has called Brother _____ to serve with us as our minister of music. Today we open our hearts to receive him and his family unto ourselves.

In so doing we place in your hands one of the most vital ministries of our church. We entrust to you our children, that under your guidance their youthful voices may come to a full knowledge and expression of the place of music in the worship and praise of their Saviour. We do not expect you to do the impossible in making sweet singers of all of us. We only ask that under your guidance we may receive a deeper appreciation for good and great music. We pray that you may help us to become known as a singing church wherein gospel music will be a true companion to gospel teaching and preaching.

As we blend our voices, hearts and hands, may they all become a symphony of service rising to the throne of grace, and making glad the heart of God.

A Minister As Civic Club Speaker

A certain American railroad some years ago adopted the policy of issuing, upon request, an annual pass to any pastor whose church was located anywhere along the railroad's right-of-way. The reasoning back of such action was that the railroad's property was no safer than the character of the people through whose communities it ran.

It is in something of the same spirit that we welcome the Reverend Mr. _____ as the speaker for our club today.

Our club is dedicated to the betterment of the entire life of our city. Thus we are co-laborers with our guest speaker. We remember the words of the Bible that man does not live by bread alone, but by every word which proceeds out of the mouth of God. What is property if it becomes an end unto itself? What value is collateral without character? Indeed, what shall it profit a man if he should gain the whole world, yet lose his soul in the bargain?

So we come to this moment, not that we should be entertained, although we most certainly shall be. We did not invite you merely to speak to our minds, though you doubtless will bring to us words of wisdom.

It is our desire that you will come to us with a message from God. We would hear from you words of eternal truth set in the context of our temporal needs. Through your presence today we would lift our souls from the pursuit of gain that we may realize the presence of God. "Where cross the crowded ways of life; where sound the cries of race and clan; above the noise of selfish strife" — through you — we would hear the voice of the Son of Man.

Our friend, our neighbor, our brother — we are in your hands!

A New Sunday School Superintendent
(Or Other Church Officer)

As we begin this new church year we are happy to welcome as the new superintendent of our Sunday school, our own Brother ———— .

You have been elected by our church to lead in this work. Your own fellow-members have expressed their confidence in you. But in so doing we realize that you cannot do this work alone. As we have challenged your leadership, so would we pledge our followship. And in so doing may we offer to you three admonitions.

First, trust in yourself. Shakespeare once wrote, "Our doubts are traitors and make us lose the good we oft might win by fearing to attempt."

But sounding another note is Ralph Waldo Emerson. "Self-trust is the essence of heroism."

Second, trust your fellow members. Emerson said, "Trust men and they will be true to you; treat them greatly and they will show themselves great."

Third, and most important of all, trust in God. "Fear [trust] the Lord, and serve him in truth with all your heart: for consider how great things he hath done for you" (I Samuel 12:24).

> One there lives whose guardian eye
> Guides our earthly destiny;
> One there lives, who, Lord of all,
> Keeps His children lest they fall;
> Pass we, then, in love and praise,
> Trusting Him through all our days,
> Free from doubt and faithless sorrow,
> God provideth for the morrow.
> —Reginald Heber

A New Associate Pastor and Family

How great is our privilege to welcome to our hearts our new associate pastor, the Reverend Mr. _____ and his family! Under the guidance of our pastor the Lord has led us to invite you and your family to become fellow-laborers in His harvest field.

Your very title expresses the relationship thus formed. As an "associate" you will be especially associated with our pastor to aid and work with him in every phase of our church life. You will be his second self as you minister with and alongside him. As a "pastor" you will, under his direction, be an undershepherd of your flock. Your ministry will be to us as one who comes from the Lord.

Our church has a great heart. As we love our pastor and his family, so will we love you and yours. Together we shall love and be loved. In the Song of Solomon we read, "and his banner over me was love" (2:4). Thus God's love in us, our love for Him, and our love for one another shall be the banner under which we shall advance to our task.

> Love is the filling from one's own
>   Another's cup;
> Love is the daily lying down
>   And taking up;
> A choosing of the stony path
>   Through each new day
> That other feet may tread with ease
>   A smoother way.
> Love is not blind, but looks abroad
>   Through other eyes;
> And asks not, "Must I give?" but
>   "May I sacrifice?"
> Love hides its grief, that other hearts
>   And lips may sing;
> And burdened walks, that other lives
>   May buoyant wing.
> Hast thou a love like this
>   Within thy soul?
> 'Twill crown thy life with bliss
>   When thou dost reach the goal.
>   —Anonymous

A NEWLY - ORDAINED MINISTER

I am happy as your pastor to welcome our newly ordained Brother _____ into the fellowship of the gospel ministry.

God never honors a church more than when He reaches down into its membership and places His hand upon one of its young men. Through the years it has been our privilege not only to lead you to the Lord but to guide you as you have grown in His favor. Thus your call to the ministry is one of God's seals of approval upon our church.

Believing that you have been called of God into His gospel ministry, our church has set you apart through ordination for this work. In so doing we have assumed a great obligation. We are obliged to pray for you, to stand by you with a helping hand, through days of preparation and beyond as you grow in usefulness for Christ.

On behalf of our church I would exhort you: "Preach the word" (II Timothy 4:2). "Endure hardness, as a good soldier of Jesus Christ" (II Timothy 2:3). "Do the work of an evangelist, make full proof of thy ministry" (II Timothy 4:5). "Take heed to the ministry which thou hast received in the Lord, that thou fulfil it" (Colossians 4:17).

So, I welcome you, my fellow-soldier, into this calling of God in Christ Jesus. It is not the easiest life which one might choose. The Apostle Paul expresses it for us. "But we have this treasure in earthen vessels, that the excellency of the power may be of God, and not of us. We are troubled on every side, yet not distressed; we are perplexed, but not in despair; Persecuted, but not forsaken; cast down but not destroyed; Always bearing about in the body the dying of the Lord Jesus, that the life also of Jesus might be made manifest in our body" (II Corinthians 4:7-10). But in it all God says, "My grace is sufficient for thee: for my strength is made perfect in weakness. Most gladly therefore will I rather glory in my infirmities, that the power of Christ may rest upon me" (II Corinthians 12:9).

Yes, it is not the easiest of callings. But it is the greatest. I welcome you, therefore, in the name of Him who placed us in the ministry!

WELCOME TO VISITORS

VISITORS IN A WORSHIP SERVICE

— 1 —

One of the most blessed moments in this hour of worship is when we pause to welcome those who visit with us.

From many places and walks of life you have come to grace our service today. Our prayer is that the Holy Spirit will so blend our hearts that we shall become one worshiping body bowed before the throne of grace.

Nearby stand our ushers to place in your upraised hands a memento of your visit with us. In this little packet you will find information to help you in becoming familiar with our church and its program. Included is a card which we trust you will fill out for us that we might become better acquainted with you. Also you will find a red ribbon to wear which will identify you to our people after the service. Thus they will be enabled to make this general welcome a personal one.

In the long ago Moses said to Hobab, "We are journeying unto the place of which the Lord said, I will give it you: come thou with us, and we will do thee good . . ." (Numbers 10:29). Yes, we will do you good, and you will do us good.

We want you to be more than visitors in our service. We invite you to become members of our family of faith. Our prayer to God for you is that today you will make our church your church, and our Saviour your Saviour!

— 2 —

The Bible speaks much of the fellowship of worship. In this spirit we welcome those who worship with us as visitors.

We are exhorted in God's Word not to forsake the assembling of ourselves together (Hebrews 10:25). In I Chronicles 16:29 we read, "Give unto the Lord the glory due unto his name: bring an offering, and come before him: worship the Lord in the beauty of holiness."

Thomas Carlyle once asked, "What greater calamity can fall upon a nation than the loss of worship?" But the need for divine worship is more than national. It is personal. The psalmist cried, "As the hart panteth after the water brooks, so panteth my soul after thee, O God" (Psalm 42:1).

You have come with your hopes and dreams, your cares and tears, your guilt and your prayers. In worship with us may you realize your fondest hopes and dreams. May your cares be removed, and your tears dried. May your guilt be cleansed, and your prayers answered.

> May the grace of Christ our Saviour
> And the Father's boundless love,
> With the Holy Spirit's favor,
> Rest upon us from above.
>
> Thus may we abide in union
> With each other and the Lord,
> And possess in sweet communion,
> Joys which earth cannot afford.
> —John Newton

Visitors in a Sunday School

A wise man once said, "A man that hath friends must shew himself friendly: there is a friend that sticketh closer than a brother" (Proverbs 18:24). It is in this spirit that we welcome you, our visitors, today.

Our deepest desire is that we shall be a friendly Sunday school. We want you to be more than visitors. We covet you as our friends. To that end we would show ourselves friendly.

In a real sense this church is our spiritual home. The welcome mat is before our portal. Even before you knock we would open the door to our hearts that we may receive you into the warmth of our love. We extend our hands in the clasp of friendship. We speak our words of greeting not as a mere formality, but with the fond hope that they may express the true pulsation of our hearts.

The primary purpose of our Sunday school is not social, yet we enjoy Christian fellowship together. It is not merely for the imparting of knowledge, though we do seek to unveil truth with the Bible as our textbook. Our primary purpose is to introduce you to our divine Friend, Jesus Christ. Some of you already claim Him as your Friend. It is our desire to help you to become a better friend as you learn and do the things which He has commanded you. For you who have never known this Friend who sticketh closer than a brother, we pray that through our friendship you will come to know Him.

Soon we shall go to our respective classes. If you have not found yours, we shall be happy to assist you to that end. The words of welcome which I speak for us collectively will soon be spoken to you by us personally. Our prayer is that when your study and worship today are ended, you will "Go home to thy friends, and tell them how great things the Lord hath done for thee . . ." (Mark 5:19).

Visitors in the Baptist Training Union

(Christian Endeavor, Etc.)

An integral part of our meeting is a word of welcome to our visitors.

The purpose of this Sunday evening gathering is that we might develop ourselves into better Christians, better church members. Meeting in small groups, we have the opportunity of fellowship as we come to know one another more intimately. But more than that we are enabled to learn by doing. Paul wrote to Timothy, "Study to shew thyself approved unto God, a workman that needeth not to be ashamed, rightly dividing the word of truth" (II Timothy 2:15).

We are saved to serve. A man can cut down a tree with a dull axe, but he can do it much better with a sharp one. So we may be more effective in our service for Christ if our minds are sharp, our hands skillful, and our hearts concerned.

Together we study our doctrinal beliefs, experience worship, improve our skills in spiritual service, and enlarge our visions as we study our missionary program. But beyond that we endeavor to engage in active service for Christ.

From this meeting we shall go together into the evening worship service. There in a larger fellowship, under the leadership of our pastor, we shall worship, pray and plead with lost souls that they may come to know our Saviour.

Therefore, we welcome you as visitors, and we do so with the fond hope that you will join with us as members of our group. Thus we shall all be enriched and encouraged in the Lord.

Visitors in the Woman's Missionary Society

We would pause to express our delight over the presence of those who visit with us today.

Donald Grant Mitchell says that a woman without religion is "a flame without heat, a rainbow without color, a flower without perfume." Contrariwise we may say that a woman with religion is a flame casting the light of God's love into the dark places of the earth, a rainbow of mingled colors shining amid the storms of this life and giving promise of God's better day, a flower whose sweet perfume of love and devotion delights the nostrils of our Heavenly Father.

When God would rear a prophet for His people He turned to a woman — Hannah. Powerful to deliver them from their oppressors He worked through a woman — Deborah. In the fullness of time when He would become flesh and dwell among us, He entered the womb of a woman — Mary. The last to view Him on the Cross and the first to declare the glad tidings of the resurrection were — women.

Luke, the author of the third gospel, was ever mindful of the place of women in the earthly ministry of Jesus. One of his most beautiful scenes is in Luke 8:1-3. As Jesus went about preaching the gospel "the twelve were with him, And certain women. . . . which ministered unto him of their substance." Each of these women had been signally blessed by Jesus. In return they sought to share His blessed ministry with others.

We would like to feel that we are in that same vein. Through our Woman's Missionary Society we endeavor to teach, promote and support our missionary work around the world. In one of his epistles Paul exhorted, ". . . help those women which laboured with me in the gospel" (Philippians 4:3).

In that spirit we welcome you into our fellowship of service. We invite you to join your lives with ours as we help you and you help us in our common labor in the Gospel.

VISITORS IN MEN'S BROTHERHOOD

Someone said that the ancient Greeks "stole" all of our original thoughts. In that sense, about 500 B.C. Aeschylus "stole" my "original" thought for tonight. Said he, "Pleasantest of all ties is the tie of host and guest." Speaking for our Men's Brotherhood, your host, to you, our guests, let me say that ours is a pleasant tie indeed.

It is the tie of fellowship, of faith, of spiritual unity. It is the tie of service rendered in forgetfulness of self and for the greater common good.

Our Brotherhood is all of these. It is built upon the belief that men like to be with men. It assumes that faith is a manly virtue. It rests upon the conviction that the spiritual unity of of kindred minds is heavenly experience in earthly surroundings.

Our Brotherhood does not exist for itself in the greater life of our church. Thus, except for an occasional project, we sponsor no program of our own. Instead, we endeavor to enlist every man in his support of every phase of our church life.

Our Lord built His work primarily about men. For it to be healthy and vigorous today it must have men at its center. We welcome you to a comradeship of Christian service. The true goal of manhood is to be a follower of Him whom the Bible calls "Jesus of Nazareth, a man" (Acts 2:22). To walk in His footsteps calls for committal, courage, conquest and sacrifice. Such a path marks the way of victorious living. To that end we welcome you. To that purpose we challenge you. In that tie we would become more than host and guest. We would be united in that indissoluble bond of Christian service as co-laborers in the Lord.

VISITORS IN MIDWEEK PRAYER SERVICE

— 1 —

In Christian love we extend our welcome to you who visit with us in this hour of prayer. Someone has said that the midweek

25

prayer service is the island of refuge upon the stormy sea which separates our Sundays. To this refuge we welcome you as we keep this sacred tryst with our Lord who said, ". . . men ought always to pray, and not to faint" (Luke 18:1).

— 2 —

It has been said that in a given church you can judge the popularity of the church by the Sunday morning congregation, the popularity of the pastor by the Sunday evening congregation, and the popularity of the Lord by the Wednesday evening congregation. We are happy to note of our visitors that although you claim neither our church nor our pastor as your own, you do claim our Lord as your Lord. We welcome you in His name!

— 3 —

Speaking for all of our people we welcome you, our visitors, into our midweek prayer service.

Victor Hugo once wrote, "There are moments when whatever be the attitude of the body, the soul is on its knees." We are doubly delighted to blend our spirits with your spirits as we bend both body and soul before our Heavenly Father.

— 4 —

Abraham Lincoln, during the darkest hours of the Civil War, said, "I have been driven many times to my knees by the overwhelming conviction that I had nowhere else to go. My own wisdom, and that of all about me, seemed insufficient for the day."

We, too, live in troubled times when naught but prayer can suffice. To this service, therefore, we welcome not only our own people but especially our visitors. Let us pray as we ought, and live as we pray.

VISITORS IN MIDWEEK CHURCH DINNER

It is with delight that we welcome our guests at this midweek dinner.

If you could truly know a family you must see it not merely when it is dressed to receive guests. You must observe it as it pursues its daily duties. A cynic once criticized the church for so great an investment in property used but once a week.

26

Such a charge cannot be made regarding our church. To borrow a thought from Shakespeare, our "task does not divide the Sunday from the week."

Tonight you see us as a family in informal fellowship about the festive board. You find us as laborers in the Lord's vineyard come together to plan and promote His work. Soon you shall join with us in the communion of prayer and praise. You shall discover us stripped of all pride and pretense as we bare our souls before God.

Wednesday night is the halfway point between Sundays. It is a time when we gird ourselves afresh for the conquest of evil in men's hearts. It is an hour when we replenish our own failing strength. It is a moment when we lift our eyes from the rugged path of daily duty and care unto the hills of God from whom cometh our help.

To such an experience we welcome you. You probably have come as the invited guest of some of us. It is our desire better to know you and to be known of you. We trust that the warmth of our welcome will radiate a like response in your heart. It is our hope that you will come again — and often. Especially do we pray that you will be with us on the Lord's Day, that you will become more than a guest, that you will join with us in our family of faith as a fellow worshiper and a fellow worker.

We have been made richer by your presence tonight. We shall be enriched indeed if you will place your heart and hands alongside ours to know and to do the will of Christ.

Visitors in General Church Dinner

Many of you have brought with you invited guests to our church dinner. We extend to each a hearty welcome.

Some of the most meaningful scenes in the life of Jesus were centered about the banquet table. So often did He attend such gatherings that His enemies called Him a winebibber and a glutton. Jesus was a social being. He knew the happy laughter and wholesome fellowship of men, women and children gathered about the festive board.

But for Him such hours were not an end unto themselves. They were means to an end. One has but to note His teachings on such occasions. One of His most meaningful pictures of heaven was that of a wedding feast (Matthew 22).

We, too, would make this hour a means to an end. This is in truth a time of worship. Moreover, it is a time of fellowship with one another. It is a time of information and inspiration.

It is a time of renewing old friendships and the making of new ones. We hope that your presence with us shall prove such a delightful experience that you will join with us in the full life of our church.

So in the name of Him who often sat at the banquet table, who sits with us even now, we welcome you.

VISITORS AMONG MILITARY PERSONNEL

We are honored to have in our service today members of the armed forces of our nation.

There is no necessary conflict between being soldiers of our nation and soldiers of the cross. The New Testament draws much on military life to express spiritual truth.

Some of our greatest military figures have been giants among the followers of Christ. The Duke of Wellington said, "The Lord's prayer contains the sum total of religion and morals." George Washington said, "Providence has at all times been my only dependence, for all other resources seem to have failed us." Robert E. Lee was a man of deep, abiding faith. On the eve of one of his greatest battles, Stonewall Jackson, a Presbyterian elder, wrote a letter to his pastor, enclosing his church contribution.

In your military service you are the watchman upon the walls of our nation. By your presence today you recognize the truth spoken by the psalmist, ". . . except the Lord keep the city, the watchman waketh but in vain" (Psalm 127:1).

So we welcome you to our service today. We shall keep you in our prayers. We shall remember your loved ones at home. And we shall strive with you as soldiers of the Lord that the Prince of Peace may reign in all nations and over all men. May the skills of war which you acquire never need to be used except in the ways of peace.

Visitors in Revival Service

A revival service without visitors would be like a treasure map in three pieces with two pieces missing. Therefore, we are especially pleased to welcome our visitors to this service.

Generally speaking, a revival meeting has a threefold purpose. It is a season of refreshing for our own members. It is a time for an unusual effort to enlist other Christians in the full life of our church. It is a period of climactic endeavor to reach the unsaved for Christ. Some of you fall in each of these three groups. To our visitors who are followers of Christ, but who have no church home in our city, we extend a cordial invitation to place your lives with us. It will bless your own lives as you strengthen ours. For other visitors who have never professed your faith in Jesus as your Saviour, we pray that tonight you will yield to the wooing of the Holy Spirit.

Someone wisely has suggested that to achieve true success in our lives, we must discover what God is doing in a given time, and throw ourselves into the adventure of doing His purpose and will. The history of religion shows that God moves mysteriously in the realm of revival movements. The English revival under John Wesley's leadership is credited with saving England from horrors such as those of the French Revolution. In America the Great Awakening turned back from her shores the deadly fog of deism and infidelity. We believe that God is moving in our day to lead us through the treacherous waters of our generation, when even the fate of civilization hangs by the slender thread of man's judgment and will.

Therefore, we welcome you, our visitors, with the hope that you will join with us in the prayer of an old revival song:

> Revive us again; fill each heart with thy love;
> May each soul be rekindled with fire from above.
> —William P. Mackay

3

WELCOME TO NEW CHURCH MEMBERS

TRANSFERS FROM ANOTHER CHURCH

— 1 —

We are happy indeed to welcome you who have presented yourselves as new members of our church. You have come from a great church to a great church.

A church is not judged by its size but by its spirit. It is not gauged by its wealth but by its willingness to fulfill God's will. In that sense we would lay claim to being a great church.

Our church is what it is today because of those who went before us. Indeed, we all are what we are because of our forebears in the faith whose blood-marked trail begins at Calvary and continues even until now. One of the greatest chapters in the New Testament is Hebrews 11. It has been called the Westminster Abbey of the Bible. After recounting the Heroes of Faith it closes with these words, "And these all, having obtained a good report through faith, received not the promise: God having provided some better thing for us, that they without us should not be made perfect."

In short, the author says that the degree of *our* faithfulness will determine the ultimate practical fruit of *their* faith. This is true whether we apply it to Christianity in its greater aspect or if we limit it to this one church.

So as a new member of our church we would point you to

> A noble army, men and boys,
>   The matron and the maid,
> Around the Saviour's throne rejoice,
>   In robes of light arrayed.

> They climbed the steep ascent of heaven
>   Through peril, toil, and pain;
> O God, to us may grace be given
>   To follow in their train!
>   —REGINALD HEBER

2

The climax of this hour of worship is in the welcoming of these new members into our fellowship. By the grace of God in Christ Jesus, and under the guidance of the Holy Spirit, you have cast your lot with us.

In receiving you we assume certain responsibilities. We pledge ourselves to minister to your spiritual needs and to those of your family. We shall endeavor to strengthen you as we keep you in the center of our prayers. We shall seek to comfort you in your sorrow, and to rejoice with you in your laughter. We shall guide you as you go on growing in the grace, knowledge and service of Christ.

But in receiving you we also place upon you great responsibilities. As one of us you will share in our privileges. You must also accept our responsibilities. A church is more than an organization. It is an organism. It will be no better than you are. Its witness waits upon your witness. Its stewardship will be limited or enhanced by the degree of your stewardship.

We place in your hands this church's good name. Wherever you go it will go. Whatever you do it will do. Men will judge your church by the degree of your consecration or lack of it. In receiving you, therefore, it is in faith that you will blend your life with ours in the service of Christ.

On behalf of our church I extend to you my hand as a token of our proffered fellowship and love, of our pledge to assume the responsibilities which you place upon us. If you, in turn, offer your fellowship and love, and accept the obligations which your coming places upon you, will you place your hand in mine?

May Christ, the Head of the church, and the Holy Spirit who indwells every believer, witness this pledge, and empower us to fulfill it!

New Christians

— 1 —

Without this moment this would be an empty hour indeed. It is a moment of hush and awe. In our midst once again the Holy Spirit has done His wondrous work. For that reason we are privileged to welcome this one as a new Christian.

In realization of and repentance from your sin you have in faith confessed Christ as your Saviour. From being dead in trespasses and sin you have come to know a new life in Christ Jesus.

Everything that we do in this church centers upon this moment. Apart from it our teaching, singing and preaching would be vain indeed. Because of your confession we place you as a trophy of grace before the Lord.

But we remind ourselves that our responsibility has just begun. A little girl, shortly after joining the church, said to her mother, "I am sorry that I joined the church." When asked why she replied, "Before I joined the church everyone was interested in me. Now no one pays me any attention."

Among the ancient Greeks and Romans unwanted babies were abandoned to die either from the elements or from wild animals. Such a practice was called *infanticide*. Even worse is the modern practice of *spiritual infanticide,* whereby we neglect those who are babes in Christ.

We must not be guilty of such. Instead, we welcome you to our hearts. We would give to you every opportunity to develop into the kind of Christian God would have you to be.

In that spirit we receive you today. Our prayer for you is found in III John 2. "Beloved, I wish [pray] above all things that thou mayest prosper and be in health, even as thy soul prospereth."

— 2 —

This is a sacred moment as we welcome to us this one who today has professed his faith in Jesus Christ as his Saviour. Like Moses we should take off our shoes, for we stand on holy ground.

Our blessed Lord said, "Ye must be born again." So before us stands one who is a babe in Christ. It is a joyful time when a baby is born into a family. But it is a joy sobered by the tremendous responsibility which God places upon the family into which the little one comes. He must be fed, clothed, loved and guided as he grows in wisdom, stature and in the favor of God and man.

Our joy just now is a sobered joy. Here is a babe who must be fed, first upon the sincere milk of the Word, and then upon the strong meat of the teachings of the Bible. He must be clothed in the garments of Christian character. He must be trained in the use of his body as an instrument of righteousness for our Lord. He must be loved with the love of Christ which is shed abroad in our hearts. He must be our constant care and concern until he grows into the full stature of Christ, until he is wise in the wisdom of God, until he receives not the favor of man alone, but of God, as one in whom He is well pleased.

So, welcome into the household of faith! You have been born again into God's kingdom. You shall be baptized into the fellowship of His church. You have not ended your spiritual pilgrimage. You have only begun it. And in the words of Sir Walter Raleigh may you say,

> Give me my scallop-shell of quiet,
> My staff of faith to walk upon,
> My scrip of joy, immortal diet,
> My bottle of salvation,
> My gown of glory, hope's true gage,
> And thus I'll take my pilgrimage.

4

WELCOME TO GUEST SPEAKERS

A GUEST MINISTER

We are fortunate indeed to welcome as our guest minister Reverend Mr. ⸺ .

John Greenleaf Whittier in his "Sunset on the Bearcamp" wrote,

> Touched by a light that hath no name,
> A glory never sung,
> Aloft on sky and mountain wall
> Are God's great pictures hung.

The Gospel is God's greatest picture. It portrays His love and grace given to a lost world. And like all great portraits, it has many facets of beauty. From each perspective it speaks a new message of God to the hearts of men.

Because of our guest today we shall view once again this portrait ever old, yet new. Through his eyes we shall see its splendors in a new light. Some hue or texture never before beheld by us will be brought into view. We will behold anew the glory of God.

May your coming to us fulfill in us the words of the Apostle Paul when he said, "But we all, with open faces beholding as in a glass the glory of the Lord, are changed into the same image from glory to glory, even as by the Spirit of the Lord" (II Corinthians 3:18).

To that end we welcome you as our guest minister, and place ourselves in your hands.

A GUEST EVANGELIST

We are happy to welcome to our church the Reverend Mr. ⸺ who will be our guest evangelist during these days of evangelistic effort.

34

This is a time for which we have prayed and to which we have given our efforts in spiritual preparation. We have publicized and organized to the end that this may truly be a time of refreshing for our souls and of witnessing to our friends and neighbors concerning the saving grace of God in Christ Jesus.

In no sense do we expect you, our guest, to bring to us a revival. We ask only that you lead us in humbling ourselves before God that He may revive us again. We shall pray for you as you preach to us. Under your inspiration we shall seek to place before you those who need to hear the Gospel that, believing it, they may be redeemed from sin and guided into a new life in Christ Jesus.

You are our guest, and we are your host. A good host will not be absent when the guest arrives. Thus we expect every member of our church to be present at each service unless providentially prevented from doing so.

This is not *your* revival, but *ours*. Since we have asked you to leave your own duties in order to help us do our work, we must take time from our daily tasks to be present at the stated services, and to go into the highways and hedges to compel through love those who should come with us.

So, welcome, our beloved brother, our comrade in a great common cause. And to you, our people would I say,

> Soldiers of Christ, arise, and put your armor on,
> Strong in the strength which God supplies through
> > His eternal Son;
> Strong in the Lord of hosts, and in His mighty power,
> Who in the strength of Jesus trusts is
> > more than conqueror.   —CHARLES WESLEY

A GUEST SOLOIST

— 1 —

With expectant joy we welcome as our guest singer for this hour Mr. ————— .

Henry Wadsworth Longfellow once wrote,

> God sent his singers on earth
> With songs of gladness and mirth
> That they might touch the hearts of men
> And bring them back to Heaven again.

35

So feel that God has sent you to us. He has endowed you with the ability to sing, and has placed a song in your heart. Through music, the universal language of the soul, God would speak to us through you. From mundane things which clog our pathway you will lead us to heaven again.

— 2 —

On your behalf I am privileged to welcome Miss ＿＿＿＿, our guest soloist for this hour.

Thomas Carlyle once wrote, "Music is well said to be the speech of angels." An angel is a messenger from God. So you are God's messenger to us. Through your ministry God will speak to our hearts. He will dry our tears, motivate our wills, and cause our spirits to mount upon the wings of song. By your presence we shall rise above the sordid things which encumber us, that we might behold the wonder and beauty of God's love and grace.

So we tune not only our ears but our hearts to your song. May it become the voice of an angel bearing in poetic loveliness the message of Him who made rhythm the guiding principle of the universe. May it be the bond between the rhythmic beat of the heart of God and the harmony of His peace within our own hearts.

An Evangelistic Singer

We are happy to welcome Mr. ＿＿＿＿ as the evangelistic singer for our revival.

Music has always played a vital part in great revival movements. The Wesley revivals needed John Wesley, but they needed his brother, Charles, also. Dwight L. Moody was a great preacher, but who can estimate the enhancing value of Ira D. Sankey in his revival campaigns? You can hardly think of Billy Sunday apart from Homer Rodeheaver.

In our revival plans we have given singing a major place, along with preaching. Indeed, the two become one in our proclamation of the Gospel. Great singing inspires great preaching, and preaching gives added meaning to the Gospel set to music.

As fire softens metal for the stroke of the hammer, so will the

36

warmth of music prepare human hearts for the preaching of the Gospel.

May your music, and ours under your leadership, quiet the deepest regions of our hearts, soften them to the impact of the Gospel, and bend them to the will of God. The Apostle Paul wrote, "I will sing with the spirit, and I will sing with the understanding also" (I Corinthians 14:15). So with spiritual fervor and understanding we await your ministry of music with and through us.

> How many of us ever stop to think
> Of music as a wondrous, magic link
> With God; taking sometimes the place of prayer
> When words have failed us 'neath the weight of care.
> Music, that knows no country, race or creed,
> But gives to each according to his need.
>
> —ANONYMOUS

A GUEST MISSIONARY

Never are we more blessed than when we have as our guest one of our Saviour's heralds of salvation to lands afar. Such is our delight as we welcome the Reverend Mr. _____ , one of our faithful missionaries.

We read in the Bible that when Paul and Barnabas returned from their first missionary journey they "gathered the church together" to rehearse "all that God had done with them, and how he had opened the door of faith unto the Gentiles [heathen]" (Acts 14:27). In a sense we are following in that apostolic succession today.

In the words of Edward Everett Hale, our guest is one of the "nameless saints." The world scarcely recognizes his worth. But he is known to us, and, most of all, to God. And when the records of eternity are revealed his name shall loom large in the plaudits of heaven.

But you, our honored guest, are not alone in this enterprise. Your work is our work. You are but an extension of ourselves in the commission of our Lord. Your stewardship of life must be equalled by our stewardship of prayer and material substance. In a sense there is no such thing as a "foreign" missionary. We are all missionaries with a message for lost people wherever

37

we are. But through you our witnessing is shod with the ten-leagued boots of the Gospel of peace.

We welcome you to our hearts at this hour. In the words spoken to Paul and Barnabas in the synagogue at Antioch in Pisidia, "If ye have any word of exhortation for the people, say on" (Acts 13:15).

A GUEST SPEAKER AT A FATHER-SON BANQUET

We are happy to have as the speaker for our Father-Son banquet, Mr. _____ . His greatest qualification is that he is both a son and a father.

How wonderful is the relationship between father and son. The expression of the eternal God stooping low to redeem is that of Father and Son. This thought places a halo about this hour.

A man is but a boy who has grown up. A son is the man he is to become. John Milton said, "The childhood shows the man as morning shows the day." There is, therefore, in this relationship a mystery which takes about it the aura of heaven.

In such a relationship there is great need for understanding between the father and the son. If we are what we should be, and our sons understand us so to be, that very knowledge is an unseen strength extended into the character of the son.

A man sought to discredit a doctor in the eyes of his son. Said he, "Did you know that your father takes sick people, straps them to a table, makes them unconscious with ether, and then cuts on them?"

The son replied, "Mister, I do not know what you are talking about, but I know my father!"

To the two-way street of such an understanding is this occasion dedicated. And your message, our beloved friend, will crown the hour. We welcome you, and place ourselves in your hands!

A GUEST SPEAKER AT A MOTHER-DAUGHTER BANQUET

This is one of the most beautiful and meaningful occasions of the year in our church. For that reason our committee was unusually careful in the choice of our speaker. Thus we are honored to have as such tonight, Mrs. _____ .

There is no human relationship so tender as that of mother and daughter. Nor is there one more important or meaningful. Someone has reminded us that if we educate a boy we educate an individual. If we educate a girl we educate a family. This is true not only of the mind but of the spirit.

Our speaker is able to appeal to both mind and spirit. She shall speak not out of books but out of experience. Her message will be not theory but fact. It will be not only what she says but what she has done.

But an effective message depends upon its hearers as well as its speaker. So we shall take into our hearts, as well as our minds, that which we shall hear. It will affect us not only as we sit together as mothers and daughters. In the broader relationship of life may your words become as shining lights along the path of the tomorrows.

We are honored by your presence. We shall be blessed by your words.

A GUEST SPEAKER AT A STEWARDSHIP BANQUET

— 1 —

We are fortunate to have as the speaker for our annual stewardship banquet, Mr. _____ . He is a man who understands this teaching, practices it in his own life, and is capable of challenging us to do the same.

The Bible says, "It is required in stewards, that a man be found faithful" (I Corinthians 4:2). Stewardship covers the whole of life. It recognizes God as the giver of life and all of its powers. It challenges us to use them for His glory. In this sense stewardship is the most widely taught of all the doctrines in God's Word.

Henry Ward Beecher once said, "Men are often like knives with many blades; they know how to open one and only one; all the rest are buried in the handle, and they are no better than they would have been if they had been made with but one blade. Many men use but one or two faculties out of the score with which they are endowed."

However, the primary purpose of this evening is that we might consider the stewardship of our possessions. Realizing that God does not really have a man until He controls all that he is and has, we are particularly facing the matter of the right use of our material substance. To that end we welcome you, our guest speaker, that you may lay upon our hearts the burden of this, the acid test of our love for God and of our obedience to His will. Through your presence tonight may we all be led to say,

We give Thee but thine own, what'er
the gift may be;
All that we have is thine alone, a
trust, O Lord, from Thee.

May we Thy bounties thus as
stewards true receive,
And gladly as Thou blessest us,
to Thee our first fruits give.

The captive to release, to God
the lost to bring,
To teach the way of life and peace,
it is a Christ-like thing.

And we believe Thy Word, though
dim our faith may be;
Whate'er for Thee we do, O Lord,
we do it unto Thee.
—WILLIAM W. How

— 2 —

We are happy to welcome as the speaker for our annual stewardship dinner, Mr. _____ .

Some of the greatest teachings of the Bible are those regarding stewardship. Knowing that covetousness is one of the most besetting of sins, a wise and merciful God has repeatedly warned against it. On the other hand, because a proper acceptance of the stewardship of life and all that it entails is the key to successful living, God has abundantly instructed us therein.

The occasion of this dinner is to remind us of the manifold elements of stewardship. Particularly it is to lead us to face our responsibility with regard to our material possessions. Soon we shall be underwriting with our pledges the work of God through our church for the coming year. Everything that we shall do, both here and around the world, depends upon what response we make.

It is extremely important, therefore, that we have the right person to speak to us tonight. It was with that in mind that we invited Mr. _____ to do so. He knows the subject, both from the teachings of the Bible and from personal experience and practice. Therefore, we place ourselves in your hands. May your coming lead us all to sing

> All things are Thine; no gift have we,
> Lord of all gifts, to offer Thee,
> And hence, with grateful hearts today,
> Thine own before Thy feet we lay.
> —JOHN G. WHITTIER

A GUEST SPEAKER IN SUNDAY SCHOOL

We are pleased to present Brother _____ as our guest speaker for this moment. Thte purpose of this period is that we might, before assembling as classes, spend a few moments in worship.

Henry Wadsworth Longfellow once wrote

> Where'er a noble deed is wrought,
> Where'er is spoken a noble thought,
> Our hearts in glad surprise
> To higher levels rise.

A part of worship is meditation. Brother _____ is well qualified to lead us in such an experience. He knows us. He knows our church. But most of all he knows the Lord.

Brother _____ , we are in your hands.

A GUEST SPEAKER IN WOMAN'S MISSIONARY SOCIETY

We are happy to have with us as our guest speaker Mrs. _____ .

Many years ago Emily Dickinson said of a woman

> To see her is a picture,
> To hear her is a tune. . . .

We may well apply these words to our guest for today.

But the picture which we see is not mere surface loveliness and grace. It is the depth and beauty of soul. The tune which

41

we shall hear is not simply the notes of a violin or the swell of a pipe organ. It is the symphony of many aptitudes and attitudes dedicated to God.

Out of the richness of your own life you have come to share with us that which the Lord has placed on your heart. We shall hear you now with pleasure and profit.

A GUEST SPEAKER AT MEN'S FELLOWSHIP DINNER

It becomes my unique privilege at this time to present as our guest speaker, Mr. _____ .

The purpose of this dinner is that men might have fellowship with men. Borrowing a thought from Arthur Davison Ficke, it is an hour when from our faces "veils pass, and laughing fellowship glows warm."

But this is more than a time of food and fellowship. It is a time of information and inspiration — a fellowship of ideas. The former is but prelude to the latter.

To that end we have invited as our speaker one who not only will entertain but inform. We did not invite him because of his fame, although we might have done so. We invited him because of his friendship, both for us and that for which we stand. Oliver Wendell Holmes once wrote

> Fame is the scentless sunflower,
>   with gaudy crown of gold;
> But friendship is the breathing rose,
>   with sweets in every fold.

So to you, our friend, we extend a hearty welcome. You will do us good.

— 1 —

The greater and more prominent the speaker the less one needs to say about him. Therefore, it is my pleasure to present to you the Honorable Mr. _____ , (mayor of our city, governor of our state, senior United States senator from our state, judge of our district court, etc.).

— 2 —

It is my great pleasure to present our speaker of the evening, the Honorable Mr. _____ .

The Apostle Paul tells us that the institution of government is ordained of God (Romans 3). Public officials are not a terror to good works, but to evil. They are ministers of God for good.

Such an one is our guest at this hour. In accepting the nomination for Governor of New York, Glover Cleveland wrote, "Public officers are the servants and agents of the people, to execute the laws which the people have made." In his presidential inaugural address he added, "Your every voter, as surely as your chief magistrate, exercises a public trust." So all of us, our guest and his host, recognize a common heritage and obligation. We are free men in whose hands have been entrusted the dignities and responsibilities of liberty.

In recognition of our trust as well as your own, we welcome you.

A Minister of Another Denomination

This is a significant hour for all of us. Sunday after Sunday we sit under the pulpit ministry of our own pastor. But today it is our privilege to have as our guest the Reverend Mr. _____ , pastor of the First _____ Church of our city. Our Heavenly Father has given us individual personalities. As such we do not all view life and its deepest meanings through the same eyes. But our hearts beat as one. In the words of John Wesley we can say, "If thy heart is as my heart, give me thy hand."

No one was ever more definite in that which he believed than the Apostle Paul. Yet he knew the broader fellowship in the Gospel which should characterize every Christian. From his prison in Rome he wrote to the church in Philippi. In the opening chapter he noted that many men preached Christ in many ways and with diversified motives.

We are children of God. We are brethren in Christ. As a family is diverse in personalities yet one in spirit, so we as children of God may find unity in diversity. Our brother in Christ is a child of God. He preaches Christ in truth, and we therein do rejoice and will rejoice.

You are our guest; we are your host. We trust that in our fellowship in Christ today, and always, you may feast upon our hospitality while we shall be fed by your words, as you become Christ's minister to us for this hour.

A Minister of Another Nationality

Happy are we to greet as our guest minister on this occasion the Reverend Mr. _____ .

One of the unique features of the Christian Gospel is that our God is not a tribal nor a national God. He is the God of all nations and all men. The fountainhead of our religion is that "God so loved the world [the inhabited earth], that he gave his only begotten Son, that whosoever believeth in him should not perish, but have everlasting life" (John 3:16).

Standing on Mars Hill in Athens, the Apostle Paul declared his philosophy of history. Central in it are his words that God "hath made of one blood all nations of men for to dwell on all the face of the earth, and hath determined the times before appointed, and the bounds of their habitation; That they should seek the Lord . . ." (Acts 17:26, 27).

The Gospel of Christ knows no national boundaries. It has crossed mountains and seas as it has surged onward in its mission which is not confined to any generation or form of human government. Its purpose is not to be conformed to any given age, but to transform men of every age. Through the ages it has lived under every type of culture and political philosophy. It has spoken to princes and peasants, servants and masters, scholars and simpletons. Its one message is, "Believe on the Lord Jesus Christ, and thou shalt be saved . . ." (Acts 16:31). Its one goal is: "The kingdoms of this world are become the kingdoms of our Lord, and of his Christ; and he shall reign for ever and ever" (Revelation 11:15).

Our guest at this hour is our fellow-patriot in the Kingdom of God. He is our fellow-soldier in the army of the Lord. Together with us his basic and ultimate citizenship is in heaven. He comes to us as an ambassador for Christ, a herald of our King.

We welcome you today as our friend, our Christian ally. We would hear your word from our Christ who is King of kings and Lord of lords!

A Minister of Another Race

It is an unusual privilege to welcome as our guest at this hour the Reverend Mr. _____ .

Standing in the house of Cornelius, a Gentile, Simon Peter, a Jew, declared, "Of a truth I perceive that God is no respecter of persons: But in every nation he that feareth him, and worketh righteousness, is accepted with him" (Acts 10:34, 35). In fact, Peter said that God does not judge a man by his face. More than anywhere else our racial characteristics appear in our faces.

Elsewhere in God's Word we read, "For man looketh on the outward appearance, but the Lord looketh on the heart" (I Samuel 16:7). When God said, "This is my beloved Son, in whom I am well pleased" (Matthew 3:17), He was not looking at the hue of His skin, the height of His cheek bones, the slant of His eyes, or the contour of His face. He was looking into the innermost springs of His soul, where in Jesus delighted to do His will always.

It is in this spirit that we welcome to us our Christian brother. The Apostle Paul summed up the matter for us. "For ye are all the children of God by faith in Christ Jesus . . . . There is neither Jew nor Greek, there is neither bond nor free, there is neither male nor female: for ye are all one in Christ Jesus" (Galatians 3:26, 28).

Our prayer today is that God through your lips will speak to our hearts His message of love and salvation to all men!

A Guest Denominational Leader

It is our signal honor to welcome to our church today the Reverend Mr. _____, executive secretary (bishop) of the Convention (Conference, Synod).

The work of our denomination is manifold and far flung in its relationships. Our churches have their particular programs and interests. But beyond the borders of the local church field looms the larger, cooperative task. Our guest is in a sense the personification of that united endeavor.

Such a person must be one of many abilities. He must be able to grace the pulpit of the largest or the smallest church. He must think in terms of the problems of the local congregation and of the field which is the world. He must be a diplomat and an administrator. He must deal in organizations but never become merely an organizer. He must be a man of vision and of practical pursuits. He must keep his head in the clouds and his feet on the ground.

Such a man is our guest today. He is the essence of the message of an anonymous poet:

> A vision without a task is a dream;
> A task without a vision is drudgery;
> A vision and a task is the hope of the world.

We look to you for a vision and a task. But most of all for this hour we look to you for a message from God.

5.

WELCOME TO CHURCH CONVENTIONS

A District or State Church Convention

It is the privilege of our church to be the host to the annual meeting of our district (state) denominational meeting. On behalf of our church may we welcome you. We place ourselves and facilities at your disposal that you may meet in comfort and convenience.

Soon we shall receive reports as to what God has done this past year through us. We trust that we shall truly give to God the glory for great things He has done. As we rejoice in His bountiful goodness to us, may we be mindful of the added responsibility which He places on us. Alexander MacLaren said, "Ability involves responsibility." Responsibility is ever the traveling companion of capjacity and power.

You have come with a serious purpose. Decisions will be made and plans initiated which will determine our witness not only here, but throughout the world. We pray that as we meet we shall be numbered by our registration cards — plus One. And that One shall be the Holy Spirit of God.

Thomas Carlyle once said, "The man without a purpose is like a ship without a rudder — a waif, a nothing, a no man. Have a purpose in life, and, having it, throw such strength of mind and muscle into your works as God has given you."

To God's people of old Isaiah delivered Jehovah's challenge. "And thine ears shall hear a word behind thee, saying, This is the way, walk ye in it" (30:21). Our prayer for this gathering is that we shall keep the ears of our souls open to hear God's voice, that we may know His will and way. When we depart may it be to walk in them.

A National Convention

As the spokesman for the churches of our city, and for its citizenry, I am privileged to welcome the _____ Convention. Ours is a city of natural beauty and friendly people. We have done all that is within our power to make your stay among us one of immediate pleasure and of lingering, fond memory.

The work of our convention encompasses not only our nation but beyond. From here we would lift our eyes over the horizon — and beyond the seas where the light of the Christian Gospel scarcely is known. We would hear the Macedonian cry, "Come over and help us!"

This is an urgent hour in the world. Modern communications have brought the peoples of the world into our very homes. Rapid travel makes the most benighted heathen our next door neighbor. The advances of material science have exceeded our fondest — and, perhaps, wildest — dreams. The destructive potential of modern nations is too terrible to ponder. But someone has said that when the world is at its worst, the Christian must be at his best.

In such an atmosphere we meet. With Paul we might cry, "Who is sufficient for these things?" (II Corinthians 2:16) However, with him we may also say, "But my God shall supply all your need according to his riches in glory by Christ Jesus" (Philippians 4:19).

My brethren,

> We are living, we are dwelling in a
> grand and awful time,
> In an age on ages telling; to be
> living is sublime.
> Hark! the waking up of nations,
> hosts advancing to the fray;
> Hark! what soundeth is creation's
> groaning for the latter day.
>
> Will ye play, then? will ye dally
> far behind the battle line?
> Up! it is Jehovah's rally; God's
> own arm hath need of thine.

Worlds are charging, heaven beholding;
   thou hast but an hour to fight;
Now, the blazoned cross unfolding, on,
   right onward for the right!

Sworn to yield, to waver, never; consecrated,
   born again;
Sworn to be Christ's soldiers ever, on!
   for Christ at least be men!
On! let all the soul within you for
   the truth's sake go abroad!
Strike! let every nerve and sinew tell
   on ages, tell for God.

—A. CLEVELAND COXE

6

WELCOME TO VARIOUS DELEGATIONS

A Delegation of Boy or Girl Scouts
(Or Other Youth Groups)

We rejoice to welcome to our service a group of Boy Scouts (Girl Scouts, etc.) and their leaders.

We are in the business of developing in boys and girls characters which are well pleasing to God. For more than a half century this has been the object of the scouting movement. It is said of Jesus as a boy, "And Jesus increased in wisdom and stature, and in favour with God and man" (Luke 2:52). This might well be the golden text of the scouting enterprise.

While not specifically told, we may assume from the gospel records that Jesus would have been a Boy Scout had such a troop existed in Nazareth. He was familiar with nature and the messages it has to teach about God. He made His body strong, His mind alert and kept His character pure. He went about doing good. He developed the skill of His hands. He had an indomitable courage. He was kind to the weak, and ever sought to lend a helping hand with no thought of personal reward.

Our church finds an ally in the scouting movement. It includes in its program the sponsorship of various units of its work. Many of our members are engaged in the broader aspects of its program.

A scout is taught to worship. So you are at home in such a service as this. We welcome you in the name of Him who said, "Suffer the little children to come unto me, and forbid them not: for of such is the kingdom of God" (Mark 10:14).

An anonymous poet wrote,

> God wants the boys, the merry, merry boys,
> The noisy boys, the funny boys,
>   The thoughtless boys;
> God wants the boys with all their joys
> That He as gold may make them pure,
> And teach them trials to endure,
>   His heroes brave
>   He'd have them be.
>   Fighting for truth
>   And purity,
>   God wants the boys!
>
> God wants the happy-hearted girls,
> The loving girls, the best of girls,
>   The worst of girls;
> God wants to make the girls His pearls,
> And so reflect His holy face,
> And bring to mind His wondrous grace,
>   That beautiful
>   The world may be,
>   And filled with love
>   And purity.
>   God wants the girls!

A DELEGATION OF PASTORS

We are happy to have in our midst a group of pastors traveling through our city, and who come to join us in this service of worship.

The Bible makes no distinction between pastors and laymen in their relation to God. We are all sinners saved by grace. But in his relation to men God has placed the pastor as an undershepherd of souls. His responsibility makes it all the more necessary that he should bow in worship before Him who placed him in this peculiar ministry.

So we welcome you as souls who hunger for a new experience with the living God. As we pray we shall lift your own congregations before the throne of grace. We shall not forget your families which are deprived of your presence. We should send you from us strengthened for the present mission upon which you are bound. We are made richer by your presence, and we pray that when you go from us you will bear happy memories of an hour when God came down our souls to greet, and His glory overshadowed the Mercy Seat.

A Delegation of Laymen

We are delighted to have in our midst a group of consecrated laymen from a sister church.

For several days they have been in our city for the purpose of studying our own church program, hoping to gain from us ideas which may be helpful to them in their own church. They have met with the pastor and the church staff. They have conferred with our deacons and with church groups charged with given responsibilities. Let me hasten to say that we have received from them more than we have given.

Your presence with us dignifies the work of the Lord. That you would leave your own business and home for this purpose speaks for your consecration to and recognition of the importance of spiritual things.

And now we climax your visit in an experience of worship. May we for this hour forget the mechanics and remember the dynamics of our service. May we be reminded that "except the Lord build the house, they labour in vain that build it" (Psalm 127:1). It is "Not by might, nor by power, but by my spirit, saith the Lord of hosts" (Zechariah 4:6).

A General Delegation
(4H, Future Homemakers, etc.)

We are honored by the presence of the _____ in our services.

From time to time it is our privilege to have various groups worship with us in a body. We are happy that you have chosen our church in which to worship.

There are many movements to aid in the development of our citizens for a richer, fuller life. And with all of them we find a common cause.

But in the experience of worship we find a unique responsibility. The churches of the Lord Jesus are peculiarly endowed with the responsibility and opportunity of developing men, women and children in the art of worship. Someone has said that if you do not worship God somewhere, you will worship Him nowhere.

But true worship is more than just one hour each week spent in a church building. It is an attitude, a way of living. It is recognizing that our souls need salvation, which can be found in Christ alone. It sees the body as the temple of the Holy Spirit. It realizes that though we may be out of God's house, we are never out of His presence.

So we welcome you in the name of Him who died, rose again, and ever liveth to make intercession for us before the throne of grace. May all of us have entered God's house to worship, that we may depart to serve!

7

RESPONSES TO WELCOMES

A NEW PASTOR

If this is a significant occasion for this church, it is equally so for me and my family. Under the guidance of God we have been led to cast our lot with you as pastor and people.

The Chinese have a saying that a journey of a thousand miles begins with one step. This one step is to welcome you to our hearts as you have opened yours to us. But the psalmist uttered an even greater truth, when he said, "Behold, how good and how pleasant it is for brethren to dwell together in unity!" (Psalm 133:1) It shall be a "unity" of love, fellowship, faith, service and purpose.

As your pastor it shall not be my purpose to drive but to lead. I do not pose as an expert in things pertaining to the spirit. I am a sinner saved by grace. As such I shall make mistakes. I shall not always live up to your expectations. But these failures, I pray, shall be of the head, and not of the heart. Thus I cast myself upon your prayerful sympathy and understanding.

This task is too great for any one mortal to perform. It calls for a community of service. One of the great words of the Bible is "fellowship." At its base it suggests sharing. So we shall share our mutual woes and burdens. Likewise we shall have fellowship in our joys. But in it all we shall heed the words of the great apostle: "For we are labourers together with God" (I Corinthians 3:9). We are fellow-laborers, and we belong to God.

> Hark, the voice of Jesus calling,
> "Who will go and work today?
> Fields are white, and harvests waiting,
> Who will bear the sheaves away?"

Loud and long the Master calleth,
Rich reward He offers free;
Who will answer, gladly, saying,
"Here am I, send me, send me"?
—Daniel March

A Former Pastor

The gracious words of welcome spoken to me by your pastor
are but another evidence of his great and generous heart. He
and I stand before you today, not as predecessor and successor,
but as friends in Christ. We are fellow-laborers in a common
cause.

By the grace of God each of us has been privileged to serve
you as Christ's undershepherd. Neither of us has done so in a
spirit of rivalry or for self-aggrandizement. It has been that we
might feed the flock of God.

The church in Corinth was disturbed over mistaken loyalties
to former undershepherds. One member said, "I am of Paul";
another said, "I am of Apollos." With Paul I would say, "Who
then is Paul, and who is Apollos, but ministers by whom ye
believed, even as the Lord gave to every man? I have planted,
Apollos watered; but God gave the increase. So then neither
is he that planteth any thing, neither he that watereth; but God
that giveth the increase. Now he that planteth and he that
watereth are one: and every man shall receive his own reward
to his own labour" (I Corinthians 3:5-8). And that reward is
from God, not from men.

So today we renew our fellowship with you, a fellowship enriched by the added presence of your pastor, my friend. May
the Lord of us all, by His Holy Spirit, blend us into a waiting
congregation, as we look to Him for His blessing.

Brethren, we have met to worship
And adore the Lord our God;
Will you pray with all your power,
While we try to preach the Word?

All is vain unless the Spirit
Of the Holy One comes down;
Brethren, pray, and holy manna
Will be showered all around. —George Atkins

55

A Minister as a Civic Club Speaker

Thank you, Mr. Chairman, for your heart-warming welcome! As I come to you today, I do not come as the Reverend Mr. _____ . I stand before you as a man, a fellow-citizen, who, I trust, comes with a message from God.

When Paul and Barnabas visited Lystra, the populace sought to welcome them as gods. To this Paul replied, "Sirs, why do ye these things? We also are men of like passions with you, and preach unto you . . ." (Acts 14:15). Some people think of the human race as composed of four genders, male, female, neuter and preachers. But preachers are men.

The favorite title which Jesus ascribed to Himself was "Son of Man." On the day of Pentecost Peter began his sermon with the statement "Jesus of Nazareth, a man . . ." (Acts 2:22). It was because Jesus completely identified Himself with man that He is enabled to be his Saviour. Only as I am identified with you may I hope to speak to your deepest heart-needs.

I would remind you, however, that as a man Jesus did not stoop to a level lower than the highest. Indeed, it is in Him that we see the goal of true manhood. Even though I fall far short of that goal, yet by His grace I stand as His messenger. And when my message is delivered, may its refrain be

> Follow with rev'rent steps the great example
> Of Him whose holy work was doing good;
> So shall the wide earth seem our Father's temple,
> Each loving life a psalm of gratitude.
> —John G. Whittier

A Guest Speaker

I am honored and humbled by your words of welcome. This is especially true because of the opportunity afforded me this hour.

One preacher asked another, "If you had but one sermon to preach, what would it be?" This question might well apply to me today. Perhaps I shall preach many times yet, but maybe to you only this one time. What, then, shall I preach?

Benjamin Disraeli once said, "The secret of success in life is for a man to be ready for his opportunity when it comes." This is an hour of opportunity for each of us. Am I ready to preach? Are you ready to hear? For both are necessary if the sermon is to achieve its intended purpose.

There is one message which surpasses all others, the story of God's redeeming love in Christ Jesus. As light passed through a prism is broken up into many colors, so this message may be seen in many rays of the reflected glory of God. Thus may our eyes behold His beauty and your hearts perceive His grace, as together we think on His Word.

A GUEST EVANGELIST

Thank you, Brother Pastor, for your gracious and meaningful welcome.

John Bunyan put into the mouth of one of his characters these words: "I will talk of things heavenly, or things earthly; things moral, or things evangelical; things sacred, or things profane; things past, or things to come; things foreign, or things at home; things more essential, or things circumstantial." But I am "determined not to know any thing among you, save Jesus Christ, and him crucified" (I Corinthians 2:2).

These are days of self-examination. So together we would search our hearts to do God's will. This is a crusade of conquest. So we would be good soldiers of Jesus Christ. Now is the time of harvest. Therefore, as laborers we would go into the field.

Standing on the battleship *Missouri* in Tokyo Bay, General Douglas MacArthur, said, "It must be of the spirit, if we would save the flesh." Ours are troubled times indeed. In calling for a revival of spiritual religion, our most earnest preachers are nuclear scientists. They but echo the centuries-old call of God to repentance and faith.

If such a revival is to come, it must begin in churches like yours. But churches are revived only as their members receive a renewal of spirit and of life. When that happens, souls will be saved and lives will be reclaimed. So my prayer is

> Lord, send a revival, Lord, send a revival,
> Lord, send a revival, and let it begin in me.
> —B. B. McKinney*

A Guest Speaker at a Father-Son Banquet

How can I thank you, Mr. Chairman, for your most generous words of welcome?

Our purpose here tonight is one of fellowship between father and son. Certainly there can be no purpose which is worthy of more serious consideration in human relationships.

Ben Johnson, the grand old Englishman, once wrote, "Greatness of name in the father oftimes overwhelms the son; they stand too near one another. The shadow kills the growth: so much, that we see the grandchild come more and oftener to be heir of the first."

But need this be the case? May not this nearness form bonds of unity instead of bars of separation? The end result lies not in proximity but in spirit. It is to this latter end that this night is dedicated.

You have honored me in inviting me to be your speaker. But you have placed upon me a greater obligation. My presence tonight will be fully compensated if thereby one father is brought to say in loving pride, "My son!" and one son says, in tender admiration, "My dad!"

A Guest Speaker at a Mother-Daughter Banquet

I shall not respond to your beautiful welcome by saying, "Madam Chairman," because such a formal address would be out of character on so beautiful and warm an occasion. Instead, I shall simply say, "My friend, I am overwhelmed by your charitable words."

As I look upon this gathering two words come to mind: beauty and love. Someone has said, "Beautiful thoughts make a beautiful soul, and a beautiful soul makes a beautiful face." James Thomson once wrote, "Loveliness needs not the foreign aid of ornament, but is when unadorn'd, adorn'd the most." It was Martin Luther who said, "Love is the image of God, and not a lifeless image, but the living essence of the divine nature which beams full of goodness."

In the light of these words, this is a sacred moment indeed. For beauty is here, and love is here. Deeper than surface adornments or passing endearments, it is the very expression of your souls. Ralph Waldo Emerson said, "Tho' we travel the world over to find the beautiful, we must have it in us or find it not."

This night is one of beauty, because it is one of love. We are not here to secure these virtues, but because they are already our possessions. But values may be enhanced. Virtues may become stronger. For these purposes this mother-daughter banquet is held.

As we contemplate this purpose, my prayer is "Let the beauty of the Lord our God be upon us" (Psalm 90:17), and may "the love of God" be "shed abroad in our hearts by the Holy Ghost [Spirit] which is given unto us" (Romans 5:5).

A Guest Speaker in Men's Brotherhood

Thank you, Mr. President, for inviting me to be with you, and for your warm words of welcome!

William Shakespeare once wrote,

> What a piece of work is man!
> How noble in reason!
> How infinite in faculties!
> In form and moving
> how express and admirable!
> In action, how like an angel!
> In apprehension, how like a god!

If you do not find yourself in that description, perhaps it is because you have not become acquainted with yourself.

It is for this purpose that we are here, that we might comprehend ourselves and God's will for our lives. Ralph Waldo Emerson said, "A man is like a bit of Labrador spur, which has not luster as you turn it in your hand until you come to a particular angle; then it shows deep and beautiful colors." Seen in the light of God, you become "deep and beautiful" indeed.

Alexander Pope spoke only a partial truth when he said, "The proper study of mankind is man." He should have added, "as God sees him." Man is made, not for one world alone, but for two. As he keeps his feet on the ground, his soul must be companion to the stars.

This truth is eloquently spoken by Thomas Carlyle. "The older I grow, and I now stand on the brink of eternity — the more comes back to me that sentence in the Catechism I learned when a child, and the fuller and deeper its meaning becomes: 'What is the chief end of man? To glorify God and enjoy Him forever.' "

A GUEST DENOMINATIONAL LEADER

Words are inadequate, Brother Pastor, as I speak to express the joy which is mine today. But I would be untrue to my own convictions if I did not say that in your most charitable welcome, you told only half of the story.

If, as you say, I am the personification of our united endeavor, then the picture is not complete until it includes each one of you. Our denominational program is your work. I am only your servant as, together, we seek to do the Lord's bidding.

In the days before we had electric motors to furnish windpower for pipe organs, this was accomplished by hand. It seems that a certain concert organist was accustomed to accepting the plaudits of his audiences, with no recognition being given, either by him or by his audiences, to the boy who pumped wind into the organ. One night the organist sat before his waiting audience to play. But when he pressed upon the organ keys, nothing happened. After several unsuccessful attempts, the organist heard a sound coming from the side of the console. Looking down, he saw the boy. With an impish grin, the boy said, "Say 'we,' mister, say 'we'!"

So I would say "we," as together we abound in the work of the Lord.

8

DEDICATIONS
New Church or Building Unit

— 1 —

One of the most solemn moments recorded in Old Testament history is Solomon's prayer of dedication for the Temple in Jerusalem (I Kings 8:22-61). Time does not permit a complete reading of this prayer, but its grandeur may be perceived in these words lifted from it.

"But will God indeed dwell on the earth? behold, the heaven and heaven of heavens cannot contain thee; how much less this house that I have builded? Yet have thou respect unto the prayer of thy servant, and to his supplication, O Lord my God, to hearken unto the cry and to the prayer, which thy servant prayeth before thee to day: That thine eyes may be open toward this house night and day, even toward the place of which thou hast said, My name shall be there: that thou mayest hearken unto the prayer which thy servant shall make toward [in] this place. And hearken thou to the supplication of thy servant, and of thy people Israël, when they shall pray toward [in] this place: and hear thou in heaven thy dwelling place: and when thou hearest, forgive" (8:27-30).

We would make this our prayer of dedication for this building which we have builded unto the glory of the Lord. Amen.

— 2 —

We dedicate this bulding to Christian fellowship. We are admonished not to forsake "the assembling of ourselves together" (Hebrews 10:25).

We dedicate it to worship. David said, "Give unto the Lord the glory due unto his name: bring an offering, and come before him: worship the Lord in the beauty of holiness" (I Chronicles 16:29).

We dedicate it to prayer. The psalmist also said, "Lift up your hands in the sanctuary, and bless the Lord" (Psalm 134:2).

We dedicate it to praise. ". . . in the midst of the congregation will I praise thee" (Psalm 22:22).

We dedicate it to preaching. Paul wrote Timothy, "Preach the the word; be instant in season, out of season" (II Timothy 4:2).

We dedicate it to evangelism. In the New Testament we read, ". . . do the work of an evangelist" (II Timothy 4:5).

We dedicate it to the development of Christian character. We are to "grow in grace, and in the knowledge of our Lord and Saviour Jesus Christ" (II Peter 3:18).

We dedicate it to God's glory. "Unto him be glory in the church by Christ Jesus throughout all ages, world without end. Amen" (Ephesians 3:21).

And we dedicate it in the name of Him who purchased the church of God with His own blood (Acts 20:28).

A PARSONAGE DEDICATION

In Deuteronomy 20:5 God asks, "What man is there that hath built a new house, and hath not dedicated it?" So we are in the will of God as we gather to dedicate this new house which our church has provided for its pastor. However, we would dedicate it not as brick, mortar, glass and lumber, but as a home.

What magic is contained in the word "home"! William Pitt said, "The poorest man in his cottage may bid defiance to all the force of the Crown. It may be frail; its roof may shake; the wind may blow through it; the storms may enter, the rains may enter — but the King of England cannot enter; all his forces dare not cross the threshold of the ruined tenement!"

Fortunately, the description is not comparable here, but the stated principle abides. What is "home" anyway? It is

> A world of strife shut out — a world of love shut in.
> The only spot on earth where the faults and failings
>   of fallen humanity
> Are hidden under the mantle of charity.
> The father's kingdom, the children's paradise,
>   the mother's world.

But home is more. A home is where tears are dried, dreams are born, and where love abides. A home, says William Cowper, is

> Domestic happiness! Thou only bliss
> Of Paradise that has survived the fall.

Or as Sir John Bowering says, "The happy family is but an earlier heaven."

A home is not a home unless God is its unseen resident. Horace Bushnell says, "A house without a roof would scarcely be a more different home than a family unsheltered by God's friendship and the sense of being always rested in His providential care and guidance."

In dedicating this house we know that it truly will be a home. So our true act of dedication will not end with this ceremony. It will continue as each of us bathes it with our love and prayer, not the building alone, but its occupants as well.

A little child with his mother walked past a house. Suddenly realizing that it was the pastor's home, he exclaimed, "God lives there!" May this ever be said of this parsonage!

An Educational Building

A building can be whatever men make it. It can be a blight or a blessing. It can be a place of sobs or of songs. It can curse or it can cure. It can edify or it can destroy.

For this reason we are gathered today for an act of dedication. Out of love and sacrifice this building has risen on the horizon of our city. But most of all it has been erected to enlarge the horizon of our lives.

The Christian religion is a teaching religion. It magnifies the mind as well as the spirit. Thus this building is dedicated to education — plus. And the "plus" is religion.

Someone has said that education without religion will fill the world with clever devils. But another has said, "Religious education should exalt and dignify the body and give a religious interpretation to the whole physical environment."

As we dedicate this building, we must dedicate ourselves to its proper use. It is not an end unto itself. It is nothing more than a tool. It will not go into all the community round about, and say, "Come ye into my halls, learn about Jesus Christ, and be saved." But it is a place to which we can invite men, women and children to come for that purpose.

In the Bible is the story of a king who made a marriage feast for his son. When everything was prepared, he sent forth his servants to say, ". . . all things are ready: come . . ." (Matthew 22:4). We stand at this point just now. We have not finished our task in religious education. We have only made ready to begin.

Therefore, from this brief ceremony let us go with the message, "All things are now ready: come . . . ."

GENERAL DEDICATION

We are assembled in a service of dedication for this ⎯⎯⎯⎯ . To dedicate means to devote, to offer or to consecrate.

Thus we would devote it. To devote means to give up wholly unto another. In this sense we give it up wholly to God. By His grace and power we have received it. He gave it to us; we give it back to Him. And as we give Him ours, we give ourselves.

Furthermore, we would offer it. To offer involves to present in worship or sacrifice. God, who made all things, does not need the work of man's hands. But we need to give it. In so doing we recognize God as the giver of every good and perfect gift. Our offering becomes our sacrifice in worship as we draw near unto Jehovah. It becomes but a token of the greater sacrifice, as we present our bodies as living sacrifices unto Him.

Likewise, we would consecrate it. To consecrate means to set apart for the service of God. Since our God needs not the gift of our hands, we can only do so as we consecrate it to His service. We serve God as we serve others. As this instrument is used in the service of others it will become God's ministry through us. By the metamorphosis of His grace it shall become a thing set apart, to the end that men shall come to know Him who made heaven and earth, and through whom we may become new creations.